MW01227402

IT GIRL
I'M THE GIRL
ITG

YOU GOT

I T GIRL

YOU CAN DO

GET

I T GIRL

YOU DID

i T girl

GOOD JOB
POSITIVITY IS THE WAY TO HANDLE

i T GiRL

REMEMBER   **TO**   **ALWAYS**

MOTIVATE YOURSELF AND YOU WILL GO FAR

Table of Contents

WELCOME THE GIRL WORLD

BEING A GIRL IS NOT ALWAYS EASY,
SO I HOPE THIS BOOK HELPS YOU.

WHEN I WAS YOUNGER, I LET NAME CALLING
MAKE ME UPSET.

I DRESSED CUTE, BUT MY ATTITUDE WAS NOT
ALWAYS POSITIVE.

I MADE GOOD GRADES, BUT I COULD HAVE TRIED
HARDER.

I WAS NOT BUILDING OTHER GIRLS UP,

I DID NOT MOTIVATE MYSELF ENOUGH.

I WAS JUST LIVING MY LIFE.

AFTER BECOMING UNHAPPY WITH THE LIFE I
CREATED,

Finally, I found myself.

I REALIZED I DID NOT WANT TO JUST LIVE MY
LIFE FOR ME.

I WANTED TO LIVE MY LIFE MAKING THE WORLD A
BETTER PLACE.

EVERYDAY, I STRIVE TO BECOME A BETTER GIRL
WHILE HELPING OTHER GIRLS FIND WHO THEY
ARE.

I WILL NEVER GIVE UP ON MY DREAMS,
BECAUSE I'M THE GIRL WHO WILL CHANGE THE
WORLD.

XO,

I T GIRL

I AM

BEAUTIFUL
SMART
AND
AMAZING.

I'M THE GIRL
THAT'S GOING TO CHANGE THE WORLD .

SO I WILL NEVER GIVE UP ON MY DREAMS.

EVERYDAY I WILL BE BETTER THAN I WAS YESTERDAY.

BECAUSE I'M THE GIRL.

THIS BOOK BELONGS TO:

_____

_____

CHAPTER 1: HEY UGLY,

Hello,
How are you today? I'm fine.
I hope your day has been going good. I see you made an A+, keep up the good work! School may not always be fun but your education is very important. So make sure you take every quiz, test, and presentation seriously. Every A+ counts, so be happy for yourself. You will not always get a congratulations from others. So the best thing you can do is be happy and encourage yourself. Being intelligent will automatically set you apart from your peers. I am here to assure you that your hardwork will pay off. So stay focused on your goals BUT don't be to hard on yourself! Do you already know one of your goals? What are you doing to reach your goals? Think about it and write it in your notebook. If you don't know what your goals are yet, it is okay. You still have time to learn and set goals. Just make sure they are

SMART

Specific • Measurable • Attainable • Realistic • Timely

If you have a goal of attending college, don't forget to apply for scholarships.

Second Languages - Sign Language - How to Budget - How to Invest - How to Network or How to Market ?

Have you ever considered learning I encourage you to look into at least one of these six things.

Now that you know, getting an education is important. I have something else important to tell you. I am not sure how you will take this but here it goes...

EVERYONE WILL NOT LIKE YOU.

I AM SORRY TO BE THE ONE TO TELL YOU THIS BUT IT IS THE

T R U T H .

There will be people who call you nice names like: BEAUTIFUL

and then you will meet people who will call you "mean" names like:

UGLY

Aren't you happy words don't hurt ?
Did you feel "Ugy" when you read the title of chapter 1 ?
💜 HEY UGLY 💜
Of course you did not, because words don't matter!
How could someone make you feel ugly, if you know for a fact you are beautiful?
That makes nooo sense!

5

Draw your IT GIRL - Draw yourself

Write your definition of UGLY

U-

G-

L-

Y-

Just because someone calls you something does not mean you have to answer!

Now that you know everyone will not like you.

I am so happy to let you know that UGLY does not have to mean the same thing for everyone. It is just a word right? Who said you could not make it mean what you want?

If I made my own meaning for UGLY it would go something like this.

UNIQUE GIFTED
LOVED YOUNG

What is your definition of UGLY?
Write it above, I know it sounds great!

Here is another meaning of UGLY

Understanding - Giving - Loyal and Yuppie

Create your defintions for words

Do not let mean words stop you from reaching for the stars.

Words are harmless so do not let them get in the way of your

GREATNESS!

You are what you say and believe you are.

6

CHAPTER 2: What's Cute?

Question:
What's a good way to
cool yourself off when you
have a negative attitude?
Meditate
and
THINK POSITIVE

IS AN ADJECTIVE THAT DESCRIBES SOMETHING.

FOR EXAMPLE: YOU ARE CUTE!

WHILE, THE COMPLIMENT IS NICE I HAVE TO LET KNOW THAT

ATTITUDE CHECK

HOW IS YOUR ATTITUDE?

☐ NEGATIVE

☐ POSITIVE

IF YOU ARE CUTE BUT HAVE A NEGATIVE ATTITUDE PEOPLE WILL NOT LIKE YOU AS MUCH AS THEY WOULD IF YOU WERE CUTE WITH A POSITIVE ATTITUDE.

WHO WANTS TO BE CUTE WITH A BAD ATTITUDE ANYWAY?

NOT ME!!

I WOULD RATHER BE CUTE WITH A POSITIVE ATTITUDE.
DID YOU KNOW YOUR ATTITUDE EFFECTS OTHERS?
BAD ATTITUDES CREATE NEGATIVE ENERGY
AND NEGATIVITY IS NOT GOOD FOR YOU,
SO TRY TO STAY POSITIVE AT ALL TIMES.

HERE ARE SOME
(———)
Negative Attitude AND *Positive Attitude*
EXAMPLES   EXAMPLES

Negative Attitude Examples	Positive Attitude Examples
• I GIVE UP!	• I WILL KEEP TRYING!
• NOONE LIKES ME.	• I AM LOVED BY GOD.
• I AM UGLY.	• I LOOK BEAUTIFUL.
• I HAVE 0 FRIENDS.	• I WILL FIND NEW FRIENDS.
• THIS IS TO HARD!	• THIS WILL TAKE SOME TIME.
• I WISH I HAD ____.	• I AM THANFUL THAT I GOT __.
• I ALREADY TRIED IT.	• I WILL TRY HARDER!
• THEY SAID _____.	• WORDS ARE HARMLESS!
• THIS IS THE END!	• MY LIFE IS JUST STARTING!
• MY DREAMS DON'T MATTER!!	• MY DREAMS WILL CHANGE THE WORLD.

DO YOU SEE HOW I CHANGED MY THOUGHTS?

Every time you are lead to a negative thought replace it with a positive thought.

For example: When I said "I give up".

That statement is not positive at all, giving up is not a option! Just because something may be hard, you still have to keep trying. How are you going to empower other girls around the world if you give up? You will not be able to and we need you! Therefore you have to encourage yourself to keep trying, so you can then encourage other girls to keep trying. I remember there were times that I felt like giving up. I had to remind myself that, i'm the girl and you needed me. So I could not give up, even if "no one" likes me, I am loved by God! If I am loved by God that means someone not only likes me, someone loves me. Which is nice to know, because then I will always have a friend.

It is the same way for you; someone loves you and will always be your friend.

So never give up! You have to keep trying!

You are the girl who's going to change the world.

8

WHILE YOU WORK ON KEEPING IT POSITIVE AND GETTING RID OF ANY NEGATVIE THOUGHTS.

YOU CAN ALSO KEEP IT CUTE BY

BEING A HEALTHY

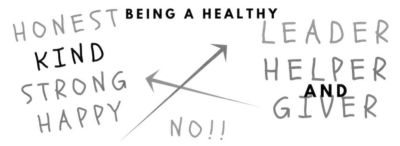

HONEST
KIND
STRONG
HAPPY

LEADER
HELPER
AND
GIVER

NO!!

YOU DO NOT HAVE TO BE ALL OF THOSE RIGHT AWAY BUT THE GOAL IS FOR YOU TO BE BETTER THAN YOU WERE YESTERDAY.

SOMEDAYS YOU WILL BE

A HONEST KIND STRONG HAPPY HELPING GIVING LEADER. OTHER DAYS YOU MAY ONLY BE A HAPPY HELPER OR A HONEST LEADER, WHICH IS STILL GOOD.

THERE IS NO SUCH THING AS PERFECT! SO, IT IS OKAY FOR YOU TO ONLY WANT TO BE HAPPY OR TO ONLY WANT TO BE KIND. THE MOST IMPORTANT THING IS THAT YOU ARE WORKING TO BE BETTER THAN YOU WERE YESTERDAY.

NOW WHEN YOU HEAR "YOU ARE CUTE". WHAT WILL YOU THINK?

9

WILL YOU FEEL PROUD?

YES!!
OF COURSE YOU WILL

WHY?? WHY?? WHY?? WHY??

BECAUSE YOU ARE CUTE. CUTE IS NOT HAVING NICE CLOTHES OR NICE HAIRSTYLES.

YOU MAKE CHOICES TO BETTER YOURSELF EVERYDAY.

YOU DO NOT ALLOW OTHERS TO INFLUENCE YOU.

YOU DO NOT JUST ACCEPT COMPLIMENTS , YOU ALSO GIVE THEM.

YOU ARE CUTE BECAUSE:

- YOU HAVE A POSITIVE ATTITUDE
- YOU ARE A LEADER
- YOU ARE A GIVER
- YOU ARE HAPPY
- YOU ARE KIND
- YOU ARE HONEST
- YOU ARE STRONG
- YOU ARE A HELPER

AND
YOU ARE HEALTHY

YOU PUT SMILES ON OTHER PEOPLE FACES . YOU HELP OTHERS REALIZE THAT THEY DO NOT HAVE TO LOOK THE BEST OR DRESS THE BEST TO BE CUTE. **YOU LET OTHERS KNOW THAT BEING CUTE MEANS YOU ARE MAKING GOOD CHOICES AND MAKING LIFE BETTER FOR EVERYONE.**

10

CHAPTER 3: Teach Me!

Wow! Wow! WOW!! You did it, you've officially made it to the final chapter. How does it feel? Are you ready to change the world? I hope so! Because you can do it, YOU ARE GOING TO DO IT! I know this a lot to take in but someday you will see the bigger picture. ⌇

Girls like YOU make the world a better place!

After a while the same people who may have called you mean names like "ugly" will be coming up to you and saying " Teach Me"! They are going to be asking you to teach them how to become

A Girl like you

What will you say? Will you tell them that you were born this way or will you teach them?

IT IS ONLY RIGHT THAT YOU

teach them!

You have your own special way of teaching. Therefore don't try and teach like someone else, you have to teach your own way. No one will know why you are the way you are BUT that is what makes you special. There is no one in the world exactly like you, so you have to be you.

11

Everyday you have a chance to learn something new that you can one day teach to someone else. It could be something as simple as how to tie your shoe, how to braid your own hair or how to love yourself. There are people all around the world looking to learn how to be happy, how to be smart, how to read, how to bake and so much more!! So what do you like to do so much that you know people would want to learn from you? Do you like caring for animals , taking pictures or making lemonade? **There are so many options, you just have to pick one.** Pick one thing you love and teach others how to love and value it.

JUST MAKE SURE YOU TRULY ENJOT IT.

Here are some ways you can learn new things on a daily basis:

Go read books at your local library.

Listen very closely to your teachers when they are teaching and take notes so you will not forget the important stuff.

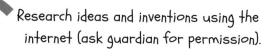

Research ideas and inventions using the internet (ask guardian for permission).

Ask guardian or trusted family member to teach you something new.

You can also learn new things by watching movies and television shows that teach you and inspire you to do better.

Success does not have to come when you are older, you can start working towards your success now. Whenever you have free time, work on something that can change the world. Create something that is so magically, every person in the world wants it.

Does that sound impossible?
You making something that billions of people want.

Yes ☐ **or** ☐ **No**

If you said yes, the answer should be no because anything is possible. It may not be a easy journey but it is not impossible.

You are capable of doing whatever you set inside of your mind, so stick to being you.
The world needs you exactly how you were created!
So do not change who you are for anyone.

BE PROUD OF HOW SMART AND INTELLIGENT YOU ARE,

Love your naturally beautiful hair and skin.

Be thankful for all of the amazing things you have been blessed with

AND
ENJOY EVERY MOMENT OF YOUR LIFE TO THE FULLEST!

REMEMBER THEY WILL BE ASKING YOU TO TEACH THEM ONE DAY, SO MAKE SURE YOU TAKE YOUR DREAMS SERIOUS AND CONTINUE TO BE YOU.
YOU ARE THE GIRL WHO IS GOING TO CHANGE THE WORLD.

**NOW THAT WE ARE DONE READING
I WANT TO MAKE SURE THAT YOU**

DON'T FORGET

YOU ARE A LEADER.

YOU WILL MAKE THE WORLD A BETTER PLACE DOING WHAT YOU LOVE.

NEGATIVE ATTITUDES CREATE NEGATIVE ENERGY.

POSITIVE ATTITUDES CREATE POSITIVE ENERGY.

EDUCATION IS VERY IMPORTANT.

MAKING GOOD GRADES CAN BRING BIG REWARDS.

YOU INSPIRE PEOPLE TO KEEP GOING.

YOUR GOALS ARE NOT IMPOSSIBLE.

GIVING UP IS NOT A OPTION.

IT IS OKAY TO GIVE COMPLIMENTS.

IT IS OKAY TO MAKE MISTAKES AND LEARN FROM THEM.

TO BE KIND AND GIVING.

TO BE HAPPY FOR YOURSELF AT ALL TIMES.

TO KEEP TRYING WHEN THINGS GET TOUGH.

YOU ARE NEVER ALONE.

ONE DAY SOMEONE WILL NEED YOU.

YOU ARE UNIQUE- GIFTED - LOVED AND YOUNG.

YOU HAVE WHAT IT TAKES TO MAKE IT.

YOU CAN BE SUCCESSFUL NOW.

YOU ARE BEAUTIFUL EXACTLY HOW YOU ARE.

KEEP THESE THINGS IN MIND AND YOU WILL GO FAR.

THE END

I'll chat with you later, don't forget the things we read about!
Luckily, you can always look back at the DON'T FORGET LIST.

Are you ready to go to work?
Flip the page for some fun & facts!

Table of Contents

ABOUT ME QUIZ

Word Search

GIRLBOSS VOCABULARY

TOP 3 GOALS

50 YEARS FROM NOW

Shine Bright Everyday

Routine

Live a life full of color

ABOUT ME QUIZ

WHO ARE YOU?

COMPLETE EACH SENTENCE
AND GET TO KNOW YOU.

My biggest dream is_____.

I love helping people with ___.

My favorite fruit is _____.

Everyday I look forward to ____.

I am happy when _____.

I inspire other people to _____.

My role model is _____.

I give back by _____.

My favorite meal is _____.

If I could do one thing forever,
I would _____.

I will change the world by _____.

One day I hope to visit _____.

UNIQUE
HAPPY
INTELLIGENT
TRUSTWORTHY
INSPIRATION
HONEST
KIND

Can you find all 17 words?

TRUTH

You Are

```
U  P  T  R  U  S  T  W  O  R  T  H  Y  I
H  R  T  C  E  E  P  G  I  A  M  D  P  H
Y  E  S  U  O  E  G  R  O  G  U  N  H  E
P  T  C  D  T  I  H  T  E  I  H  I  E  A
P  T  H  A  S  L  U  O  L  E  Y  K  N  L
A  Y  O  E  E  Y  A  N  I  R  E  M  O  T
H  H  K  E  N  I  S  H  I  T  A  O  M  H
F  R  P  U  O  N  R  B  R  Q  N  N  E  Y
P  U  I  E  H  E  T  T  N  D  U  H  N  D
T  N  E  G  I  L  L  E  T  N  I  E  A  E
A  I  N  S  P  I  R  I  N  G  G  C  L  V
B  E  A  U  T  I  F  U  L  K  K  U  E  O
A  I  V  W  Q  K  G  S  M  A  R  T  I  L
A  L  D  A  T  A  E  R  G  F  T  E  E  S
```

I AM
GORGEOUS
PRETTY
UNIQUE
INSPIRING
BEAUTIFUL
INTELLIGENT
PHENOMENAL
HEALTHY
KIND
TRUSTWORTHY
CUTE
GREAT
HONEST
HAPPY
LOVED
SMART

Remember, YOU ARE WHAT YOU SAY YOU ARE!

As you learned in the book, if you speak and think positive,
positive things will come your way. All around are words
that positively describe who you are.

Everyday pick a word and be happy about who you are.

I AM
BEAUTIFUL
PRETTY
SMART
GORGEOUS
POSITIVEGREATLOVED

HEALTHY
CUTE

VOCABULARY

AMBITIOUS - STRONG DESIRE TO SUCCEED

ATTAINABLE - REALISTIC AND CAN BE REACHED

ATTITUDE - FEELINGS ABOUT SOMETHING

BEAUTIFUL - HIGH STANDARDS WITH A GOOD HEART

DETERMINED - DECIDED TO DO SOMETHING
NO MATTER WHAT IT TAKES

EMPOWER - INSPIRE OTHERS TO DO BETTER

FEARLESS - BRAVE AND FREE FROM FEAR

GIFTED - SPECIAL TALENT OR ABILITY

GIVER - PERSON WHO GIVES SOMETHING

GOAL - SOMETHING YOU WANT IN LIFE

HEALTHY - PHYSICALLY FIT AND BALANCED EMOTIONS

HONEST - TELLING NO LIES

INSPIRATION - GIVES YOU A NEW IDEA OF SOMETHING TO DO

INTELLIGENT - ABILITY TO LEARN AND UNDERSTAND NEW THINGS EASILY

LEADER - ABILITY TO MAKE SOMEONE MORE CONFIDENT AND STRONGER

LOVED - NEVER ENDING CARE OR CONCERN

MEASUREABLE - CAPABLE OF BEING TRACKED AND MONITORED

MEDITATE - SIT QUIETLY , BREATH SLOWLY AND THINK POSITIVE

NEGATIVE - LOW ENERGY, MEAN AND RUDE

PHENOMENAL - CONFIDENT IN YOU AND YOUR DREAMS

POSITIVE - HIGH ENERGY,NICE, AND GIVING

SPECIFIC - CLEAR UNDERSTANDING

SUCCESS - ACCOMPLISHMENTS THAT MAKE YOU PROUD AND HAPPY

TIMELY - CAN BE ACHEIVED BY A SET DATE

UNIQUE - ONE OF A KIND

YUPPIE - YOUNG PROFESSIONAL

TOP 3 GOALS

IF YOU WANT TO REACH A GOAL YOU HAVE TO
SAY IT – WRITE IT – SET A DATE & REACH IT.

GOAL #1

GOAL #2

GOAL #3

I WOULD LIKE TO REACH GOAL #1 BY:
_____
I WOULD LIKE TO REACH GOAL #2 BY:
_____
I WOULD LIKE TO REACH GOAL #3 BY:
_____
IF I WANT TO REACH GOAL #1 I WILL HAVE TO:
_____
IF I WANT TO REACH GOAL #2 I WILL HAVE TO:
_____
IF I WANT TO REACH GOAL #3 I WILL HAVE TO:
_____
WHY ARE THESE GOALS IMPORTANT TO YOU?
_____

IF YOU KEEP TRACK OF YOUR GOALS YOU WILL BE
ABLE TO ACHIEVE THEM **EASIER AND QUICKER**.

SHINE BRIGHT EVERYDAY

January · Feburary · March · April · May · June · July · August
· September · October · November · December

1	2	3	4	5	6	7	8
9	10	11	12	13	14	15
16	17	18	19	20	21	22
23	24	25	26	27	28	29	30	31

YEAR _____

TO DO LIST
-
-
-
-

MY GOAL TODAY IS:

_____

_____

MY MOOD TODAY WAS

TODAY I
- [ ] HELPED SOMEONE
- [ ] ADMIRED NATURE
- [ ] MADE MYSELF SMILE
- [ ] KEPT TRYING

QUESTIONS OF THE DAY?
· HOW MUCH WATER DID I DRINK TODAY?
· DID I EXERCISE TODAY?

TODAY
- [ ] WAS GREAT
  OR
- [ ] COULD HAVE BEEN BETTER

50 YEARS

Step 1: Draw your head shape. • Step 2: Create yourself a beautiful hairstyle.
Step 3: Draw your pretty gorgeous eyes, nose, eyebrows, eyelashes, lips and teeth.
Step 4: Give yourself shoulders or a body.
If you would like to add a body, continue to step 5.
If you only want to add shoulders, add shoulders and continue to Step 7.
Step 5: Draw your arms, legs, feet and fingers. • Step 6: Dress yourself in something FABULOUS.
Step 7: Color your future self.

In 50 years from now life will be so much different, cars may be floating or technology may be gone.
Sounds crazy right? Although it sounds crazy it is the truth.
Life will not be exactly how it is today,which is why you have to make a positive difference in the world.
One day the world will need your talent, leadership skills, beauty and brains.

So how will you be looking 50 years from now?
Will you be looking like you did 50 years ago?
Or will you look like 50 years have passed?

The answer is up to you.

Will you not worry about harmless mean words?
Will you keep trying when things get hard?
Will you drink your water and exercise on your own?
Will you keep being the best you can be?
Will you help someone become a better person one day?

If you answered yes to those 5 questions,
50 years from now everyone will be asking you what's your secret.

Funny thing is, you are just a girl who decided to make herself and the world a better place.
In 50 years, I will have:

_____
_____
_____
_____
_____

What all will you have did that you will be proud of in 50 years?

ROUTINE

THE BEST WAY TO ENSURE YOU ARE
REACHING YOUR FULL POTENTIAL
IS TO CREATE A ROUTINE.
A ROUTINE CAN BE DONE ON A DAILY,
MONTHLY OR YEARLY BASIS.
YOUR ROUTINE SHOULD BE CREATED TO
WORK FOR YOU AND AROUND YOUR LIFE.
A EXAMPLE OF A DAILY ROUTINE IS :

WAKE UP
PRAY
BRUSH TEETH
WASH FACE

IF YOU DO THIS EVERY MORNING AND
NIGHT, THIS IS A ROUTINE.
AS TIME GOES BY YOU HAVE THE ABILITY TO ADD
TO YOUR ROUTINE OR TAKE THINGS OUT OF YOUR
ROUTINE. YOUR ROUTINE IS COMPLETELY UP TO YOU.
HERE ARE 3 SMALL YET IMPACTFUL THINGS
THAT CAN BE ADDED TO YOUR ROUTINE:

GIVE BACK
MAKE SOMEONE SMILE
OFFER A HELPING HAND

THEY MAY NOT SEEM LIKE MUCH BUT YOU WILL
MAKE A DIFFERENCE IN THE WORLD. YOU ARE
THE GIRL WHO WILL MAKE THE WORLD A
BETTER PLACE. LEARN HOW TO LOVE YOURSELF
AND SPEAK LIFE INTO YOURSELF. WAKE UP
THANKFUL TO BE ALIVE EVERYDAY. TELL
YOURSELF YOU ARE AMAZING, YOU ARE
BEAUTIFUL, YOU ARE STRONG, YOU ARE HEALTHY,
YOUR LIFE MATTERS AND YOU ARE IMPORTANT.
I HOPE THIS BOOK TAKES YOU EVEN FUTHER
THAN YOU WERE ALREADY GOING TO GO

TOP

COLOR ME

SPREAD PEACE·SHARE LOVE·CREATE HAPPINESS

PEACE   LOVE   HAPPINESS

EACH PAGE YOU JUST READ OR COMPLETED WAS CREATED TO HELP YOU GROW.

AS TIME GOES BY THINGS WILL MAKE EVEN MORE SENSE TO YOU. MAKE SURE YOU COME BACK TO REREAD YOUR BOOK AND UPDATE YOUR ANSWERS. WRITE ON THE PAGES IN THE BOOK AND WRITE IN A NOTEBOOK. YOUR NOTEBOOK CAN BE USED ON A DAILY BASIS TO WRITE DOWN YOUR THOUGHTS , IDEAS, GOALS AND YOUR DAILY TASKS.

I HOPE YOU LEARN HOW TO YOU USE THIS BOOK TO GET THROUGH THE OBSTACLES THAT LIFE WILL BRING YOUR WAY. THIS BOOK WAS DESIGNED TO INSPIRE YOU AND INFORM YOU THAT YOU ARE SOMEBODY IMPORTANT. YOUR LIFE MATTERS AND ONE DAY YOU WILL MAKE HISTORY.

IN LIFE THINGS WILL NOT ALWAYS SEEM LIKE THEY ARE GOING YOUR WAY BUT THEY ARE. LIFE IS ALWAYS WORKING OUT FOR YOUR GOOD EVEN WHEN IT LOOKS LIKE IT IS NOT. AS YOU GET OLDER YOU WILL LEARN THAT LIFE IS NOT ABOUT HOW YOU LOOK OR BEING BETTER THAN SOMEONE. LIFE IS ABOUT HELPING OTHERS UNDERSTAND THAT THEY HAVE A PURPOSE.   LIFE IS ABOUT BEING THANKFUL FOR THE SMALLEST GIFTS AND LOVING YOUR NATURAL SELF.

REPEAT AFTER ME:
I'M THE GIRL WHO WILL CHANGE THE WORLD ONE DAY AND
I WILL NEVER GIVE UP ON MY DREAMS BECAUSE MY DREAMS MATTER.

IF YOUR SKIN IS
BREAKING OUT
DRINK MORE WATER AND
TAKE A BREAK FROM
SWEETS AND MEATS.

CAN'T STOP THE SWEAT?
TRY MAKING HOMEMADE SOAP
USING THINGS LIKE ALOE VERA,
FRESH CHAMOMILE TEA,
LAVENDER, TEA TREE OIL, WITCH
HAZEL AND MORE

HEY GIRL WHO WILL CHANGE THE WORLD ONE DAY,
I AM HONORED THAT YOU READ MY BOOK.
Never forget that you can have and do anything positive in life. You
just have to believe that you can actually have or do it.
If you have any doubt, the magic it will not work.
You have to truly believe in yourself.

See you at the top!

HOW MUCH WATER SHOULD YOU
DRINK EVERYDAY?

DIVIDE YOUR WEIGHT BY #2
THAT WILL GIVE YOU THE OUNCES.
DIVIDE THE OUNCES BY #8 AND THAT
WILL GIVE YOU THE NUMBER OF CUPS
OF WATER YOU SHOULD DRINK
EVERYDAY.

FEELING SICK?
GET SOME REST FIRST
AND
ONCE YOU ARE FEELING
BETTER
DO A LIGHT EXERCISE.

WHAT DID YOU
EAT TODAY?
DID YOU HAVE
YOUR
CARBS- FIBER-
PROTEN AND FAT

HAVING A BAD DAY?
TAKE 30 MINUTES OR LESS TO
CHECK YOUR ATTITUDE. DO NOT
ALLOW YOUR BAD DAY TO BE
BAD FOR LONGER THAN 1 HOUR.

ABOUT THE AUTHOR

GRADUATED
ENTERPRISE HIGH SCHOOL,
RECEIVED HIGH SCHOOL DIPLOMA

2018

2019
PUBLISHED FIRST BOOK
"I'M THE GIRL"

2007

BORN

1996

2014

GRADUATED
JERRY LEE FAINE ELEMENTARY,
RECEIVED
RAMARLA MUSSELMAN AWARD

GRADUATED
ALABAMA STATE UNIVERSITY
RECEIVED
BACHELORS OF SCIENCE IN
MANAGEMENT

ASHUNTAE SMITH WAS BORN AND RAISED IN ENTERPRISE, ALABAMA. SHE HOLDS A B.S. IN MANAGEMENT, A TESOL CERTIFICATION, AND A SUBSTITUTE TEACHING LICENSE. ASHUNTAE HAS WORKED WITH OVER 100 CHILDREN SINCE GRADUATING FROM ALABAMA STATE UNIVERSITY. SHE HAS SUCCESSFULLY TAUGHT CHILDREN HOW TO SPEAK PROPER ENGLISH AND SHE IS COMMITTED TO INVESTING INTO OTHERS.
IN ADDITION TO TEACHING, ASHUNTAE IS ALSO A ENTREPRENEUR SPECIALIZING IN HAIR BRAIDING, T-SHIRT DESIGNING, EVENT PLANNING, GIFT MAKING AND MORE. SHE IS WORKING TOWARDS HER DREAM OF OPENING HER OWN STOREFRONT IN HER HOMETOWN. SHE LOVES HELPING OTHERS FIND WHO THEY ARE AND TEACHING THEM THE VALUE OF MAKING POSITIVE DECISIONS. ASHUNTAE ENJOYS MAKING NEW MEMORIES, CREATING NEW PLANT-BASED MEALS AND FINDING
NEW WAYS TO GIVE BACK TO THE WORLD.

Made in the USA
Columbia, SC
20 March 2024